# FRIENDS
# OF ACPL

P9-CND-515

## DO NOT REMOVE
## CARDS FROM POCKET

# Hidden Underneath

# Hidden Underneath

*Kim Taylor*

Delacorte Press

Published by Delacorte Press
Bantam Doubleday Dell Publishing Group, Inc.
666 Fifth Avenue, New York, New York 10103
This work was first published in Great Britain
in 1990 by Belitha Press Limited.
Text copyright © Kim Taylor 1990
Photographs copyright © Kim Taylor and
Jane Burton 1990
Consultant: Ellen Fader

Manufactured in Great Britain
September 1990
10 9 8 7 6 5 4 3 2 1

Library of Congress Cataloguing-in-Publication
Data

Taylor, Kim.
  Hidden underneath/Kim Taylor.
    p. cm. – (Secret worlds)
  Summary: Describes a variety of animals and
their habitats, including the porcelain crab,
partridge, and digger wasp.
  ISBN 0-385-30180-4.
  ISBN 0-385-30181-2 (lib. bdg.).
  1. Zoology – Juvenile literature. 2. Camouflage
(Biology) – Juvenile literature. [1. Animals.] I.
Title. II. Series: Taylor Kim. Secret worlds.
QL49.t225   1990
591.56'4 – dc20                        89-78281
                                            CIP
                                            AC

*I*F YOU TURN OVER A STONE OR A FALLEN LOG ALMOST anywhere, you will find interesting things underneath it. Even dead leaves lying under a tree have animals living beneath them. A green leaf often has aphids clinging to its underside. In the picture (*opposite*), there is a mother aphid with all her daughters. They are sucking juice out of the leaf. Soon the daughters will start to give birth, so the mother will be a grandmother.

You have to be very lucky to find a tree frog underneath a leaf (*above*). It has special pads on the ends of its toes, which it uses to cling safely to the leaf.

*A flake of bark*

WHEN THE BARK STARTS TO COME LOOSE FROM A DEAD tree, it makes a safe home for many different sorts of animals. This flying gecko (*above left*) hides under a flap of bark during the day and comes out at night. This one is a female and has laid two eggs. Where bark begins to peel away and a wide gap appears, brown creepers find enough space for a nest (*above right*). The picture shows the mother bringing earwigs to feed her babies, which have grown so big that they have climbed out of the nest onto the underside of the bark.

When a tree dies, there is a soft layer under the bark that starts to rot first. Click beetle larvae (*above left*) feed on this layer, which is damp and makes good food for them. Their bodies are flattened and they fit neatly between the bark and the trunk of the tree. Whip scorpions (*above right*) are also flattened so that they can fit into narrow cracks. They often live under dry bark and come out at night to feed. They feel their way with long thin feelers, like whips, and catch insects with their spiky arms.

## Stones on land

*U*NDERNEATH STONES THERE ARE HOMES FOR MANY different animals. This lump of brick and concrete (*opposite*) has been turned over to show some sowbugs and a centipede hiding. They stay there, where it is dark and damp, during the day but creep out to feed in the safety of the night. The slug eggs (*above left*) were found in damp soil under a mossy stone. If they were left in the open, they would soon dry up and die. In warm countries, you might find a scorpion under a stone (*above right*). Be careful—scorpions have a dangerous sting!

## Stones on the seashore

TURNING OVER STONES ON A ROCKY SHORE IS INTER-esting but you should always put them back very gently. Otherwise the animals stuck to the underside of the stones will die. Some kinds of fish stay underneath the stones when the tide goes out. They find little puddles of water or damp seaweed to lie in. They can even breathe air through their skins while they wait for the tide to come in. This eel was hiding under a stone, along with two starfish (*below left*). The scorpionfish (*below right*) is in a pool under a stone on an African beach. Like scorpions, scorpionfish have dangerous stinging spines.

Some seashore animals also cling to the undersides of stones. These porcelain crabs (*below left*) are very flat, so that they can fit into narrow cracks. One fell on its back when the stone was turned over and is showing its white underside. Porcelain crabs filter little bits of food out of the water with special feathery arms.

The star-shaped things stuck to the stone near the crabs are called ascidians. They also filter food. A bread-crumb sponge is another sort of animal found sticking to stones (*below right*) and it, too, filters food. All these filter feeders help to keep seawater clean.

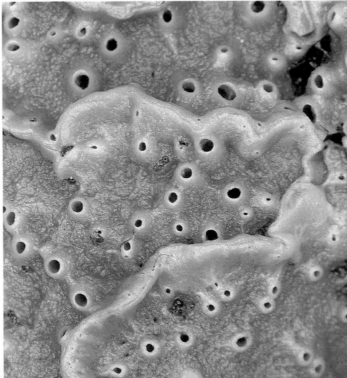

*Under the sand*

*E*VEN A SANDY SHORE HAS LOTS OF ANIMALS LIVING ON it—and under it! European masked crabs (*above*) bury themselves in the sand until only their feelers are sticking out. When something tasty drifts past in the water, a masked crab grabs it with its pincers. Soldier crabs live on the sandy beaches of warm countries. They walk about in armies after the tide has gone out, filtering food out of the sand and spitting out clean sand in little pellets. If you come close to an army, the soldiers just disappear into little sandy igloos, like the one opposite.

## Underneath an anemone

MOST ANIMALS DON'T LIKE TO GET TOO CLOSE TO a sea anemone for fear of being caught by its tentacles. But some animals have learned to swim among the tentacles without getting caught. They even take their names from their partnership with anemones. They hide underneath the anemone, using it as a sort of umbrella. The clown anemone fish (*below right*) is safe from other fish when it stays underneath its big umbrella. And the anemone shrimp (*opposite*) does a good job picking bits off its anemone to keep it clean. But the hermit crab (*below left*) takes *its* anemones for a ride wherever it goes.

*Underneath a sitting bird*

*A* GRAY PARTRIDGE IS SITTING ON ITS NEST IN THE LONG grass. She is well hidden and keeps perfectly still. Her feathers are fluffed out to keep the eggs underneath her warm. She has laid an egg every one or two days until the clutch is complete. Now she must sit there for twenty-four days until all the eggs hatch. Underneath her, everything is just right for the eggs: it is warm and damp, and there is enough air passing through her feathers for the eggs to breathe. Yes, eggs do breathe through their shells!

Of course, the sitting partridge has to feed and stretch her legs occasionally. When she gets up, the nest is much easier to see because of the pale-colored eggs. There are fourteen of them. If it is a warm day, the mother bird may spend some time away from the nest, but if it is cold, she returns quickly so that the eggs do not get chilled. When she returns, she may turn the eggs over with her beak. This makes it easier for the chicks inside to hatch.

*Under fur and feathers*

FEATHERS ARE GOOD FOR KEEPING A BIRD WARM AND dry, but nasty creatures can get underneath them. The louse fly (*opposite*) has a flattened body and walks sideways like a crab. When it lands on a bird, it quickly scuttles underneath the feathers where the bird cannot catch it. Birds hate louse flies because they suck blood, and they panic when they see one coming. Fleas also suck blood and have flattened bodies so that they can easily pass between the hairs of a furry animal. If you were as small as this cat flea (*above*), passing through cat fur would be like walking through a forest!

## *Underwings*

MOTHS HAVE FOUR WINGS, A LARGE PAIR ABOVE AND a smaller pair underneath. The large forewings are often dull in color so that the moth is difficult to see when it is resting during the day, like the eyed hawk moth of Central Europe (*above left*). When the moth raises its forewing, a large "eye" appears on the underwing (*above right*). When an emperor moth (*opposite*) is disturbed by a bird, it raises its forewings suddenly and the bird is surprised and frightened by the two big eyes that appear.

*Beneath the house*

A BASEMENT IS A ROOM BENEATH A HOUSE. IT STAYS cool in the summer and warm in the winter. A basement is often unused, and so it stays quiet and is a good place for animals to rest. Eight herald moths and one small tortoiseshell butterfly spent all winter clustered together on the ceiling of a basement. One spring night the moths all flew out, and in the morning, when the sun was shining, the butterfly went as well.

Because basements are underground, they are often damp inside and are good places for fungi to grow. This dry rot fungus has spread across a basement floor. It has grown out like a fan from a single piece of wood. The fungus is searching for more wood in which to grow. Dry rot fungus causes a lot of damage in houses. It can quickly cause a strong piece of wood to crumble. The best way to stop dry rot is to make sure that all the wood in a house is kept dry.

*Underground flowers?*

*I*T SOUNDS ALL WRONG FOR A PLANT TO HAVE AN UNDER-
ground flower, but some plants do. In parts of Africa,
cracks in the ground have beetle trap flowers in them.
These smell horrible to us, but beetles rush to them and
fall in. The beetles cannot climb out until the flower dies;
and when they *do* come out they are covered in pollen,
and soon fall into the next beetle trap. A plant called
aspidistra, which people grow in their houses, also has
underground flowers that attract ground-living insects.
The flowers are meant for beetles, not bees!

## *Underneath the ground*

$A$ S YOU WALK OVER THE GROUND, YOU DON'T HAVE any idea of what is going on beneath your feet. Only occasionally can you see signs. Heaps of sand show where some animals have been digging, and you can sometimes see the holes that they have made as well. The small sand heaps (*above left*) are made by digger wasps. They catch other insects to provide food for their grubs which live in the burrows. The wasps sometimes build a little castle of sand at the entrance of their burrows. One is looking out from its castle (*above right*).

Earthworms also build little heaps of earth called *casts*. This is soil that they have swallowed and then passed out. They dig their burrows by eating the soil and they get their food from it as well. In some places you can find lots of earthworms gathered together, like these in a compost pile (*below left*). Moles build much bigger heaps of soil, which they push up from their underground tunnels. They eat any earthworms that drop into their tunnels, first pulling the worm through their front feet to clean the dirt from it (*below right*).

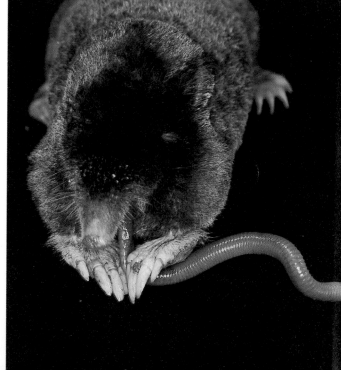

# Index